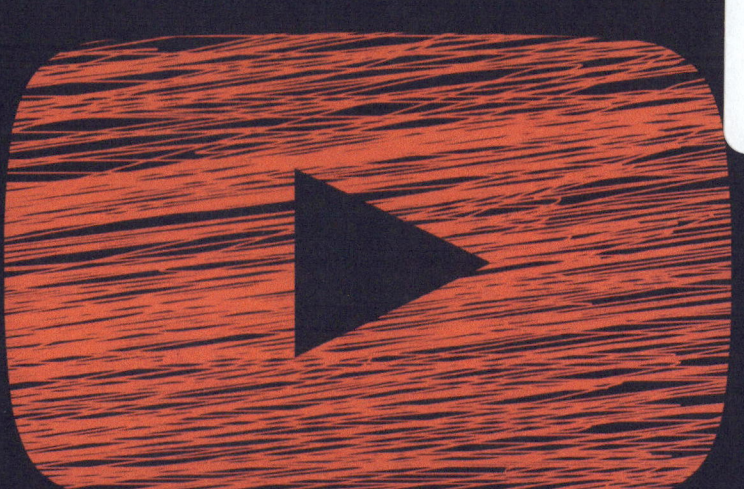

THE YOUTUBE GAMING MASTERCLASS

Build A Successful Gaming Channel In 2020

MOHAMEMD KASMI

Table of Contents

I. Introduction

II. Setting up the channel

III. Some examples of gaming videos you can create

IV. How To Get 1000 Subs And 4000 Hours Quickly

V. How To Edit Your Videos And Reach More Viewers

VI. SEO Tactics

VII. Conclusion

INTRODUCTION

Hello there, welcome to this ebook, where you will learn everything you need to know to create a successful gaming YouTube channel.

We will tackle subjects such as your channel's initial set up, niche selection, how to get people to watch your content, and some tips on how to edit your gaming videos for maximum audience retention.

By the time you complete this ebook, you will have amassed a base of knowledge that will help you build a successful gaming channel and reach your dreams.

We will begin by taking a look at some of the most frequent questions people ask before starting a YouTube channel, then we will move to channel setup.
From there we will talk about which kind of videos you should be making.
And finally, we will talk about SEO and how to rank your videos well on search.

I hope you are ready to start your journey as a gaming YouTuber.

IS YOUTUBE GAMING STILL PROFITABLE?

This is a question asked by many people, more so recently since the latest YouTube terms of service update and the Coppa law, as that made people super anxious of starting a YouTube channel .

But should they be ?

Sure, The Coppa law sucks but should you decide not to start a YouTube channel because of it ? I personally think that Gaming on YouTube is still profitable and anyone who says otherwise is fooling you.

Sure some creators might suffer from Coppa, especially games that attract a lot of children but that doesn't mean that all games are doomed.

But, keep in mind that I am in no way a lawyer or able to give you legal advice, but there are a lot of Experts out there even on YouTube who are talking about Coppa, and they can give you a better understanding than I ever can.

VIDEO RECORDING METHODS

There are two methods to how you can record your gaming footage:

"software recording" and *"hardware recording"*

- Software recording is using software to record footage. There a lot of softwares that can record in this way such as OBS/Bandicam, but by using this method you will often see a drop in FPS.

Usually it's not that significant, and softwares nowadays have lowered the FPS drop to a point where it's not even noticeable.

Also, it's worth mentioning that most of these softwares are free.

- Hardware recording, allows you to record more smooth footage with no FPS drops whatsoever, but, it is more expensive than software recording, which makes it a bad choice for beginners.

I hope you got an idea on how to record your footage now, if I were to recommend something I'd recommend OBS as it is a very stable software used by professionals and beginners alike, and it's also open source.

MICROPHONES FOR RECORDING

When talking about microphones you will find two types :

"USB Microphones" and *"XLR Microphones"*

so which one should you get ?

Which one is better ?

Well, as a rule of thumb, if you have a big budget then you should definitely get an XLR microphone as they are better than USB microphones.

But as a beginner, or if you don't have enough money to invest in an XLR Microphone, then just get a decent USB Mic.

That's it for our introduction, next we will begin with how you should set up your channel in a way that will make it easy to grow fast

SETTING UP THE CHANNEL

CHOOSING THE NICHE / SUB-NICHE

You see before even thinking about creating a YouTube channel you need to sit down and think really carefully about your *"TARGET AUDIENCE"*

Most new YouTubers tend to fail because they don't understand the importance of choosing a niche and a target audience.

I can't emphasize this enough, choosing a niche is the most important thing that you need to think about before you even think about making videos.

So why is choosing a niche so important ?

by choosing a niche and making content around it you will start getting targeted viewers who eventually could turn into subscribers and loyal fans.

So if you grow a channel making GTA V videos, but suddenly start making League of legends videos, you will notice that your videos are now getting less views!

and you know why ?

CHOOSING THE NICHE / SUB-NICHE

Maybe your audience doesn't like League of Legends,

so you lost a huge amount of viewership simply because they lack interest in the new content you make.

In short, people always want to watch what they signed up for, In this example that would be GTA V videos.

So now that you understand why choosing a niche is important, we can dive deeper and talk about sub-niches

You see, every niche has many sub-niches inside of it

For example : In the case of GTA V some possible sub-niches are GTA V machinimas or GTA V funny moments.

The concept here is that after you pick a niche you will work on, most of the times you have to pick a sub-niche that is not super saturated.

Why should you do that? well, one thing : *"Less competition"*

spend some time thinking about your *"Target Audience"* as this is a very important part of creating a successful channel.

CHANNEL ART & LOGO

You can use any software you want to make your channel art.
I personally use Photoshop but you can use any software you want.

I won't be going into details about designing the Art as this book is not about that, but I will be giving you some tips on what to add in your designs.

while designing your channel art you need to keep in mind to add a few key elements, you can for example add your schedule to make it easy for new visitors to know exactly when you will be uploading.
You can also use your channel art to promote your products.

I mean really, the possibilities are endless but just don't crowd the channel art with too much information, otherwise, it will be overwhelming to your viewers.

The same also goes for the Logo, choose a simple design that you want to be known for and once you make something that you are proud with, you can then use it as your Logo.

Think about your Logo as the face of your channel, so you ought to make a good design that you would love to show to other people.

BRANDING AS A KEY TO GROWTH

Branding is how you differentiate yourself from everyone else, whether that be how you edit your videos, or the way your thumbnails look, even how you speak.

Branding will help you gather a loyal fanbase, or as some call them super fans.

Those are people who are so loyal to you and will watch and engage with most of your content.

And it's those kind of fans that you want to gather because those are the ones likely to check your offers and potentially buy your merch/products.

You need to start working on branding since the beginning of your channel as its effects will start showing later on.

CREATING THE ABOUT PAGE

In the about page of any YouTube channel you will find a description and some links at the bottom.

the channel description is super important because it will allow people to have some information about your channel that you couldn't add in the channel art or simply needed more space to explain it.

You will also find a place to add a business email, this is important because this is how companies who are interested in working with you will be contacting you.

if you don't have an email prepared then you will lose on so many opportunities that you could have gotten.

Lastly there are the links, and this is where you put links to your websites.

Any website you want to promote should be added into this section, and the links you add will appear in the top right hand corner of the screen above the subscribe button.

WHY MAKE A SCHEDULE ?

It all comes down to consistency and habit, you want to educate your audience to comeback each Thursday for example to watch one of your videos.

and by doing this you will not only increase views from subscribers, but as more of your subscribers return to watch more of your content, YouTube will begin promoting your video more and now you will start attracting new viewers who would potentially subscribe to you.

So, how many videos should I upload per week ?

Many people agree that the minimum is 1 or 2 videos per week, and as a beginner that is fine because you don't want to upload a lot of trash content just for the sake of uploading as that will do more harm than good to your channel.

As a rule of thumb, choose a schedule based around your time, don't forsake your mental health, trust me, you will not be able to keep making videos after a while of forcing yourself. Especially if your content doesn't work out.

BONUS TIP

"Using Upload Defaults"

If you use the same title/description/tags over and over again,
what you can do is save your description as an upload default and whenever you upload a new video your description will be automatically added and this way you will save a lot of time.

II

Gaming Videos Examples

WHICH VIDEO TYPE TO MAKE ?

There are a lot of video types you can make, but, you should definitely spend some time thinking about this, and you should not skim over it because believe me when I say, it is as important as choosing a niche.

Why is that ?

because it comes down to what you love making, and what you're passionate about.

If you force yourself to make videos that you don't like, people will notice and call you out on it, and most of them would stop watching you altogether.

There is a nice phrase that summarizes this point :

"If you don't care about your content, why should I ?"

You see what I mean right ?

So please spend some time to think about what videos you really love to create.

WHICH VIDEO TYPE TO MAKE ?

As there are lot of video types, i cant cover them all in this book,
So I'm going to give you a few of the most known gaming video types :

- Let's Play
- Walkthroughs
- First Impressions
- Montages
- Reviews
- Long plays
- Funny Moments
- Highlights
- Machinimas

III

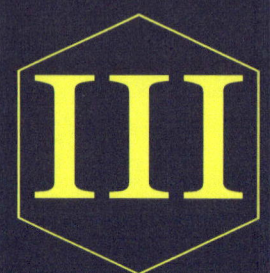

How To Get 1000 Subs And 4000 Hours Quickly

USING LIVESTREAMS TO REACH 4000 HOURS QUICKLY

Think about this for a second :

The average livestream is 1 hour long.

so why not use that to your advantage?

Especially if you are a gamer!

why not do a livestream at least twice per week.

Think about how many hours you will get by just streaming games.

So the more you stream the more hours you get

a simple equation.

ADDING CLEAR CALL TO ACTION STRATEGICALLY THROUGHOUT THE VIDEOS

You need strategic call to actions, don't just start blasting "subscribe now graphics" throughout your videos.

That will actually deter people from subscribing.

And don't put a subscribe graphic at the very last second of your video, you will lose on so many viewers who didn't make it that far in the video.

Instead, focus on putting the graphics in moments where you believe there isn't much going in the video, for example if you make a montage video, you could add a transition like a "fade out" the moment a song ends, and then ask people to subscribe.

If you make a let's play, you can add a subscribe CTA whenever there is a peaceful moment, and nothing much is happening.

Those are just some examples about when you can place a CTA in your videos.

As it is really case sensitive I can't give you a specific time where you should put a CTA.

IV

How To Edit Your Videos And Reach More Viewers

THE 3 PHASES OF A YOUTUBE CHANNEL

Every channel has phases in its lifetime, and in general YouTube channels have 3 phases :

0-100 subscribers :

Now this is truthfully one of the hardest barriers to pass as a

You Tuber, don't be fooled. It's very hard to generate traffic to your channel. At this stage you can't even use Reddit to promote your videos, Reddit folk generally tend to upvote less when they see it's a video with no likes/comments/views.

Also it's nice to have subscribers upvoting for you, regardless of how big the subreddit is.

So where do you get traffic?

First off we have social media, and by that I don't mean your personal Facebook, but more so Facebook pages and Twitter users.

Try to find a demographic, specifically for the type of content you make. For us gamers especially it's very easy, there's always these very niche Fb/Twitter pages for just the type of content you make.

You can Tweet at people/pages, and that's a very solid way of achieving traffic to your channel. I know for a fact that many Facebook pages also accept submissions.

THE 3 PHASES OF A YOUTUBE CHANNEL

Now why do I only mention Facebook/Twitter, well when it comes to social media there's no denying that they're the biggest, and the best.

Networking extends far beyond this, and joining a YouTube community like yttalk is a great way to meet people and grow your channel.

But I'm just mentioning these as examples.

What else can factor into the super early growth? Well I HATE to say this, however how fast you grow also depends a lot on luck. Take 2 channels who both have great similar content, one of them may just have a video that ends up in many suggested video boxes, and in turn gives them more traffic.

You can't always know which tags will be best for your video, however if you keep at it you should get there eventually.

I don't suggest promoting yourself in YouTube comment section, it drives more trolls and haters to your channel than actual followers.

100-1000 subscribers :

THE 3 PHASES OF A YOUTUBE CHANNEL

Now it's time to start your growth-train, and to start you off you need something big, something better, you NEED gateway video(s).

Now what is a gateway video? I've mentioned them several times before.

basically they are widely appealing, short, entertaining videos, That give people an incentive to subscribe.

A gateway video, can be ANYTHING you make as long as you make sure it fulfills these 3 requirements :

1 - Your video MUST be entertaining, there's no other way to put it.

If people watch a video and they don't like it, well then they're just moving on.

I can't give any more advice to this step, since entertainment has so many forms, and how you want to embody that in your videos is your choice.

2 - Your video must give people an incentive to subscribe, but fret not, this DOESN'T mean you have to make a series of videos that are super similar.

If you can manage to give people a reason to subscribe, other than asking them to do so, then you are on your way to gateway growth.

THE 3 PHASES OF A YOUTUBE CHANNEL

3 - keep it short, now this isn't a requirement as much as it is a guideline. There are plenty of longer gateway videos out there, however being straight to the point and not dragging things out, will generally please a larger audience.

1000-selfsustainable stage :

Your goal from 1000 subscribers is basically to reach a point where your channel will grow on its own without you promoting it. And by grow, I mean visible growth in between each video.

And the most powerful sentence that I'm sure will help any YouTuber out there :
"Make everything better than the previous".

It's honestly the best advice I think one can give, and even if you try and fail, that doesn't matter. Everyone has their highs and their lows.

The smug YouTuber will look at a channel that's bigger than his/hers, and say "My content is better, this guy/gal is so lucky that he/she is so big".

The smart YouTuber will look at a channel that's bigger than his/hers, and say "Wow this channel sure has a lot of followers, instead of looking at what I do better than them, let me look at what they do better than me, and learn from that"

THE 8 SECONDS RULE (THE HOOK)

What is The Hook ?

The hook is as the name suggests a hook for your viewers.
How do you plan on hooking your viewers and enticing them to watch the whole video.

There are many ways you can hook viewers, like asking a question in the beginning of the video, showing a preview of an interesting part in the video or previewing the end result of the video, and building towards that result.

Those are just examples, and based on your video you decide on how to hook your audience, and keep in mind :

As a rule of thumb the first 8 seconds of your video should be dedicated to the Hook.

You need to hook your audience as soon as the video start and you have 8 seconds to do that, so make those 8 seconds count.

TARGETING THE RIGHT KEYWORDS

Before even beginning to edit your videos you need to run some research, and try to find the best keywords for your videos.

I personally use Tubebuddy in my research :

By using Tubebuddy you can look for keywords by using the "Keyword Explorer" and finding the best keyword.

You need to choose a keyword that does not have as much competition, and that's searched enough (You don't want to target keywords with very low search volumes as nobody will be there to watch your content)

"Here's a tip :" When choosing your keywords, try to find a keyword that has an amount of monthly searches, extra points for finding one with low competition as that will definitely up your chances of getting more views.

After finding your keywords, it's time to actually write your title and description.

FOCUS ON YOUR VALUE PROPOSITION

Now you should have an idea about how to make videos that people want to watch.

But how to keep them watching?
And how to turn them into subscribers?

You should also be focusing on the value you provide.
What is your value proposition?
Why should anyone subscribe to you on YouTube?

For example, if you make Let's Play videos, your value proposition could be your personality, you could communicate to your audience that they should subscribe because they can hang out with you and then you start building a kind of personal relationship with your viewers, which is always nice to have.

Another example could be if you make montage videos, and this time your value proposition could be that they should subscribe to you because you make awesome montages.

Sometimes the value proposition is the video itself, so keep that in mind.

V

SEO Tactics

WHY THUMBNAILS MATTER A LOT

Thumbnails are one of the most if not the most important aspects of driving viewers to your videos.

Thumbnails are like movie posters, the better they are the more people will click on them.

There are a lot of tips on how to make your thumbnails clickable and no they are not all about design, as you can find many thumbnails with really simple designs outperforming ones with really complex designs.

What you should keep in mind is that thumbnails should be enticing, so try to play around the need of your potential viewer. if you make League of Legends montage videos don't make a thumbnail showing different champions, instead stick to the champion you're making the montage about.

Also some say that thumbnails with a human face tend to work more than thumbnails with only text or design.

All in all, you should experiment with different thumbnails and see what works best for your channel.

WHY TITLES ARE SO IMPORTANT

Titles are so important in getting views because they are the thing that will hook most of your viewers, in addition to your thumbnails of course.

And that's why many successful YouTubers spend a lot of time crafting their titles.

Because titles are the key to increasing views.

So you might be asking yourself, how do I write a great title? Well, first of all you should write your title based around the keyword research you made before.

Try to get as many keywords in the titles, with the most important keywords near the beginning of your title, but, make sure that your title is readable by humans. Don't blast all your keywords there and make a mess.

Reason why, your video won't rank and YouTube might demote your video because of spam.

So take your time when crafting a title, because that's the first clue for your viewers on what the video is all about.

If you can craft a title that attracts viewers to watch your video, then you just struck gold.

Here's a few tips on how to craft a killer title :

WHY TITLES ARE SO IMPORTANT

- ❑ See what your competitors are doing with their titles, and see what works for them, and what doesn't.
- ❑ Make sure your title is readable
- ❑ Make sure your title is the correct size, don't go over 70 characters
- ❑ Try to make a title that entices people to watch the video, but don't clickbait them

Thank You For Finishing My Ebook

Don't waste anymore time start making the videos you love
go out there and crush it!!

www.ingramcontent.com/pod-product-compliance
Lightning Source LLC
Chambersburg PA
CBHW041935240526
45473CB00034B/1708